AF414963

What follows is a list of all the reasons the keto diet does not work...

All the science-backed evidence why Keto doesn't work...

All the science-backed evidence why Keto doesn't work...

All the science-backed evidence why Keto doesn't work...

All the science-backed evidence why Keto doesn't work...

All the science-backed evidence why Keto doesn't work...

All the science-backed evidence why Keto doesn't work...

All the science-backed evidence why Keto doesn't work...

All the science-backed evidence why Keto doesn't work...

All the science-backed evidence why Keto doesn't work...

All the science-backed evidence why Keto doesn't work...

All the science-backed evidence why Keto doesn't work...

All the science-backed evidence why Keto doesn't work...

All the science-backed evidence why Keto doesn't work...

All the science-backed evidence why Keto doesn't work...

All the science-backed evidence why Keto doesn't work...

All the science-backed evidence why Keto doesn't work...

All the science-backed evidence why Keto doesn't work...

All the science-backed evidence why Keto doesn't work...

All the science-backed evidence why Keto doesn't work...

All the science-backed evidence why Keto doesn't work...

All the science-backed evidence why Keto doesn't work...

All the science-backed evidence why Keto doesn't work...

All the science-backed evidence why Keto doesn't work...

All the science-backed evidence why Keto doesn't work...

All the science-backed evidence why Keto doesn't work...

All the science-backed evidence why Keto doesn't work...

All the science-backed evidence why Keto doesn't work...

All the science-backed evidence why Keto doesn't work...

All the science-backed evidence why Keto doesn't work...

All the science-backed evidence why Keto doesn't work...

All the science-backed evidence why Keto doesn't work...

All the science-backed evidence why Keto doesn't work...

All the science-backed evidence why Keto doesn't work...

All the science-backed evidence why Keto doesn't work...

All the science-backed evidence why Keto doesn't work...

All the science-backed evidence why Keto doesn't work...

All the science-backed evidence why Keto doesn't work...

All the science-backed evidence why Keto doesn't work...

All the science-backed evidence why Keto doesn't work...

All the science-backed evidence why Keto doesn't work...

All the science-backed evidence why Keto doesn't work...

All the science-backed evidence why Keto doesn't work...

All the science-backed evidence why Keto doesn't work...

All the science-backed evidence why Keto doesn't work...

All the science-backed evidence why Keto doesn't work...

All the science-backed evidence why Keto doesn't work...

All the science-backed evidence why Keto doesn't work...

All the science-backed evidence why Keto doesn't work...

All the science-backed evidence why Keto doesn't work...

All the science-backed evidence why Keto doesn't work...

All the science-backed evidence why Keto doesn't work...

All the science-backed evidence why Keto doesn't work...

All the science-backed evidence why Keto doesn't work...

All the science-backed evidence why Keto doesn't work...

All the science-backed evidence why Keto doesn't work...

All the science-backed evidence why Keto doesn't work...

All the science-backed evidence why Keto doesn't work...

All the science-backed evidence why Keto doesn't work...

All the science-backed evidence why Keto doesn't work...

All the science-backed evidence why Keto doesn't work...

All the science-backed evidence why Keto doesn't work...

All the science-backed evidence why Keto doesn't work...

All the science-backed evidence why Keto doesn't work...

All the science-backed evidence why Keto doesn't work...

All the science-backed evidence why Keto doesn't work...

All the science-backed evidence why Keto doesn't work...

All the science-backed evidence why Keto doesn't work...

All the science-backed evidence why Keto doesn't work...

All the science-backed evidence why Keto doesn't work...

All the science-backed evidence why Keto doesn't work...

All the science-backed evidence why Keto doesn't work...

All the science-backed evidence why Keto doesn't work...

All the science-backed evidence why Keto doesn't work...

All the science-backed evidence why Keto doesn't work...

All the science-backed evidence why Keto doesn't work...

All the science-backed evidence why Keto doesn't work...

All the science-backed evidence why Keto doesn't work...

All the science-backed evidence why Keto doesn't work...

All the science-backed evidence why Keto doesn't work...

All the science-backed evidence why Keto doesn't work...

All the science-backed evidence why Keto doesn't work...

All the science-backed evidence why Keto doesn't work...

All the science-backed evidence why Keto doesn't work...

All the science-backed evidence why Keto doesn't work...

All the science-backed evidence why Keto doesn't work...

All the science-backed evidence why Keto doesn't work...

All the science-backed evidence why Keto doesn't work...

All the science-backed evidence why Keto doesn't work...

All the science-backed evidence why Keto doesn't work...

All the science-backed evidence why Keto doesn't work...

All the science-backed evidence why Keto doesn't work...

All the science-backed evidence why Keto doesn't work...

All the science-backed evidence why Keto doesn't work...

All the science-backed evidence why Keto doesn't work...

All the science-backed evidence why Keto doesn't work...

All the science-backed evidence why Keto doesn't work...

All the science-backed evidence why Keto doesn't work...

All the science-backed evidence why Keto doesn't work...

All the science-backed evidence why Keto doesn't work...

All the science-backed evidence why Keto doesn't work...

All the science-backed evidence why Keto doesn't work...

All the science-backed evidence why Keto doesn't work...

All the science-backed evidence why Keto doesn't work...

All the science-backed evidence why Keto doesn't work...

All the science-backed evidence why Keto doesn't work...

All the science-backed evidence why Keto doesn't work...

All the science-backed evidence why Keto doesn't work...

All the science-backed evidence why Keto doesn't work...

All the science-backed evidence why Keto doesn't work...

All the science-backed evidence why Keto doesn't work...

All the science-backed evidence why Keto doesn't work...

All the science-backed evidence why Keto doesn't work...

All the science-backed evidence why Keto doesn't work...

All the science-backed evidence why Keto doesn't work...

All the science-backed evidence why Keto doesn't work...

All the science-backed evidence why Keto doesn't work...

All the science-backed evidence why Keto doesn't work...

All the science-backed evidence why Keto doesn't work...

All the science-backed evidence why Keto doesn't work...

All the science-backed evidence why Keto doesn't work...

All the science-backed evidence why Keto doesn't work...

All the science-backed evidence why Keto doesn't work...

All the science-backed evidence why Keto doesn't work...

All the science-backed evidence why Keto doesn't work...

All the science-backed evidence why Keto doesn't work...

All the science-backed evidence why Keto doesn't work...

All the science-backed evidence why Keto doesn't work...

* 9 7 9 8 6 0 3 0 0 1 7 6 0 *